Contents

1 Who were the Tudors and Stuarts? 4

2 Then and now 6

3 How religion changed 8

4 What was town life like? 14

5 Elizabethan country life 20

6 Entertainment in Shakespeare's time 26

7 How transport changed 32

8 The privateers: heroes or pirates? 38

9 Why did the Armada fail? 42

10 Was Guy Fawkes framed? 46

11 How did people fight in the Civil War? 50

12 Life in Pepys' London 54

13 Plague! 56

14 Fire! 60

Index 64

HENRY VII m. Elizabeth of York
(1485–1509)

Arthur   HENRY VIII   m. 1. Catharine   2. Ann Boleyn   3. Jane Seymour
(died)   (1509–1547)   of Aragon

EDWARD VI
(1547–1553)

MARY I
(1553–1558)

ELIZABETH I
(1558–1603)

Key

m. =   married

(1509–1547) = years as king or
                queen of England

▬▬▬   Tudors

▬▬▬   Stuarts

How the Crown was passed on

When a monarch died his, or her, eldest son became king. If he died the next eldest son became king. When there were no more sons left the crown was passed to the oldest daughter, and then down the rest of the daughters by age.

So, when Henry VIII died the crown went first to his only son, Edward; then to his eldest daughter, Mary; then to his youngest daughter, Elizabeth.

Tudor and Stuart Times

Jane Shuter

Adam Hook

Judith Maguire

HEINEMANN
EDUCATIONAL

Heinemann Educational
a division of Heinemann Educational Books Ltd
Halley Court, Jordan Hill, Oxford OX2 8EJ

OXFORD LONDON EDINBURGH MADRID
ATHENS BOLOGNA PARIS MELBOURNE
SYDNEY AUCKLAND SINGAPORE TOKYO
IBADAN NAIROBI HARARE GABORONE
PORTSMOUTH NH (USA)

First published 1992

97 96 95 94 93
10 9 8 7 6 5 4 3

**British Library Cataloguing in Publication
Data** is available from the British Library on
request.

Designed by Ron Kamen, Green Door Design
Ltd, Basingstoke, Hants

Printed in Hong Kong

Acknowledgements

The authors and publisher would like to thank
the following for permission to reproduce
photographs:

Bodleian Library: 4H, 7F
Bridgeman Art Library/
   Belvoir Castle, Leicestershire: p.4 (*Henry VIII*)
   Bristol Museum and Art Gallery: 3B
   Christie's London: p.4 (*Henry VII*)
   Private Collection: p.4 (*Elizabeth I*)
   Society of Antiquaries, London: p.4 (*Mary I*)
   Roy Miles Gallery: p.5 (*James I*)
   Victoria & Albert Museum: p.5 (*James II*)
   Trustees of the Weston Park Foundation: p.5
   (*Charles I*)
British Film Institute: 11G
British Library: 3C, 5L, 8F, 14K
Viscount Coke and the Trustees of the Holkham
Estate: 5I

Devonshire Collection, Chatsworth. Reproduced
by permission of the Chatsworth Settlement
Trustees: 6A
Library of Congress, Washington D.C: 10D
C.M. Dixon: 11D
By permission of the Folger Shakespeare
Library: 3I
Freer Gallery of Art, Smithsonian Institution,
Washington D.C: 7J
Fotomas Index/Marquess of Salisbury: 2A
Trustees of the Geffrye Museum: 4D
Michael Holford/British Museum: 3A
Hulton-Deutsch Collection: 4A, 6J
Mansell Collection: 10C, 13D, 13H
Museum of London: 7D, 14A, 14E
National Maritime Museum, London: 7G, 9A,
9C, 9F
National Portrait Gallery: 3D, 6C, p.4 (*Edward
VI*), p.5 (*Charles II*), p.5 (*Mary II, William III* and
Queen Anne)
National Trust Photographic Library/John
Bethall: 5E
New College, Oxford/Philip Parkhouse: 10F
Pepys Library, Magdalene College, Cambridge:
12A
Royal Collection, St James's Palace © Her
Majesty the Queen: 7C
Society of Antiquaries of London: 3F
Jamie Stamp: 2B
Victoria & Albert Museum: 7I
Bob Watkins: 2C
Weidenfeld & Nicolson Archives: 3G

Cover photograph shows Baron Cobham and
his family. Reproduced by permission of the
Marquess of Bath.

Our thanks to Mike Mullet of the University of
Lancaster for his comments in the preparation
of this book.

1 Who were the Tudors and Stuarts?

Margaret m. 1. James IV   2. Archibald   Mary
           of Scotland   Douglas

James V
of Scotland

Margaret m. Matthew Stuart

Mary Queen   m. 1. Francis II   2. Henry Lord
of Scots   of France   Darnley

JAMES VI of Scotland
also JAMES I of England (1603–1625)
m. Anne of Denmark

Henry   CHARLES I   m.   Henrietta Maria   Elizabeth
(died)   (1625–1649)   of France   m. Frederick of Germany

CHARLES II   JAMES II m. 1. Anne   2. Mary
(1660–1685)   (1685–1688)   Hyde   of Modina
m. Catherine of Braganza

MARY II   m.   WILLIAM III of Orange   ANNE
        (1689–1702)   (1702–1714)

2 Then and now

The Tudors and the Stuarts reigned for over 200 years.
The last Stuart monarch, Queen Anne, died nearly
300 years ago. There are ways in which the people who
lived in England then are very different from us today. But
there are also ways in which they are the same.

Source
A

A picture of a wedding in Bermondsey
in about 1592.

Source B

A wedding
in Bermondsey
in 1992.

Source C

Bermondsey in 1992.

How did things change?

If you look at Sources A and C, you can see that London has changed a lot. Bermondsey is not a village any more, it is part of London. The fields have gone, the buildings are now high brick-built ones, the roads are paved.

The only thing that is still the same is that the Tower of London is still there, almost hidden by Tower Bridge. If you look at Sources A and B, you can see that people's clothes have changed. People still get together to celebrate weddings. They wear their best clothes, and eat together.

3 How religion changed

In 1485 England was a Catholic country. Everyone went to church on Sunday. They all heard the same service, in Latin. Most of them would not have understood the service.

In 1530 Henry VIII was king. He wanted to have a son to be king after him. His first wife had many babies. But only one girl lived. Henry wanted to end his marriage and marry again. Catholics could not do this easily. Only the **Pope**, as Head of the Catholic Church, could give permission to end a marriage. Henry asked the Pope to do this. The Pope said no. So Henry made himself Head of the English Church, instead of the Pope, and got a **divorce**.

Parliament agreed to the change. Some people agreed because they wanted Henry to marry again. Some agreed because they thought the Catholic Church was too powerful and rich. These people wanted to **reform** the Church, to make the people in it think more about God, and less about power and money.

Henry started the **reformation** of the Church. He inspected the abbeys, whose monks and nuns were said to be very rich and not very religious. He closed the abbeys down, and took their money for himself.

Source A

Many of the monks go hunting and shooting. The prior is often drunk.

The abbess cannot read, nor can any of her women.

The prior likes to play dice, and spends a lot of money on this.

Three of the reports from the people who inspected the abbeys.

Source B

This painting shows the closing down of Syon Abbey in 1539. It was painted about 300 years after it happened.

Source C

This picture of a monk drinking wine comes from a decorated book. Monks had been accused of drunkenness for centuries.

Source A is a list of the things that were wrong with the abbeys. The people who were sent to inspect the abbeys were told only to report on what was wrong with them.

Reports that had been made on abbeys in earlier times were different from the ones like Source A.

Firstly, they had been made by church people, for the Church, not by ordinary people for the King.

Secondly, they were not done at the same time all over the country.

Thirdly, they were reports on everything that was happening in the abbeys.

They reported on the good things, as well as the bad things.

Inspectors like the ones who wrote Source A would have left the good things out. It was not what they had been sent to find out about.

The **Reformation** made people think about how they really wanted to worship. **Catholics** wanted to worship in the same way they always had. **Protestants** wanted to go back to the way people worshipped in the Bible. But they could not agree about how this should be done. So there were many different sorts of Protestantism. Some Protestants thought that people should worship God very simply. They were called **Puritans**. The **official** religion (the one the government wanted people to use) kept changing.

Source **D**

1547–1553: Edward VI was a Protestant and wanted everyone else to be Protestant too. He had the first Prayer Book in English made. He stopped all Catholic services. The soldiers in this picture are pulling down Catholic statues.

Catholics and Protestants

People on both sides of the argument over religion were sure they were right. They believed that people only went to Heaven if they worshipped God in the **right way**. This is why they were willing to be burned for their beliefs. They would rather be burned on Earth than burn in Hell forever, which is what they thought would happen.

Source **E**

1553–1558: Mary was a Catholic. She wanted to make sure that everyone in the country became Catholic. This picture shows Protestants being burned for not becoming Catholics in the reign of Queen Mary I.

**Source
G**

1625–1714: England stayed a Protestant country. After the Civil War (when there was no king or queen) the government was very Protestant. It even banned Christmas! There were worries about Catholic plots all through the period. But by the time of Queen Anne people were sure enough that England would stay Protestant to make fans like this one to celebrate.

**Source
F**

1558–1625: Elizabeth I was a Protestant, so she changed the Catholic ways brought in by her sister, Mary I. But she did not want to force everyone to have one religion. As long as people went to church, or open-air services like the one in the picture, she did not worry about how they worshipped in their own homes. Things settled down and carried on in the same way into the reign of James I.

Catholics and Protestants

Catholics wanted:

- The Pope as Head of the Church.
- Services in Latin.
- Lots of statues, ornament and paintings in churches.

Most Protestants wanted:

- No Pope.
- Services in English.
- Plain churches.

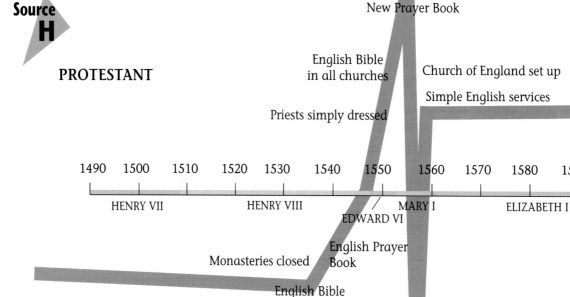

PROTESTANT

New Prayer Book

English Bible
in all churches

Church of England set up

Simple English services

Priests simply dressed

| 1490 | 1500 | 1510 | 1520 | 1530 | 1540 | 1550 | 1560 | 1570 | 1580 | 1590 | 1600 |

HENRY VII   HENRY VIII   MARY I   ELIZABETH I

EDWARD VI

English Prayer
Book

Monasteries closed

English Bible

CATHOLIC

Mary burnt
Protestants at the
stake because of
their religion.

By 1714 the official religion of Britain had changed many times. Services were now in English, and people could follow them in their Bible and Prayer Book. But, despite all the changes, some things were the same. Almost everyone still believed in God. They were still Christians. They still went to church on Sunday. They still marked the important days in their lives (like births, weddings and deaths) with church services.

Puritans wanted:
- Very plain churches.
- A table in the middle of the church, not an altar.
- Sunday as a day for God, no games or other enjoyments.

How did things change?

If you look at Source H you can see that:

Religion changed most **rapidly** (quickly) between 1536 and 1560.

Religion changed most **gradually** (slowly) between 1560 and 1610.

The change which probably had the biggest effect on people was holding services in English. Now people could understand what was going on.

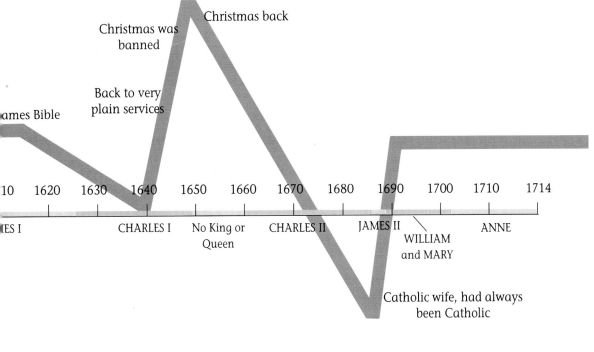

Christmas was banned

Christmas back

Back to very plain services

ames Bible

| 10 | 1620 | 1630 | 1640 | 1650 | 1660 | 1670 | 1680 | 1690 | 1700 | 1710 | 1714 |

ES I

CHARLES I   No King or Queen   CHARLES II   JAMES II   ANNE

WILLIAM and MARY

Catholic wife, had always been Catholic

▼ A painting on a church wall, from about 1500. It shows the Last Judgement when people were sent either to heaven or to hell. Pictures were used to show the most important ideas from the Bible, as the services were in Latin which most people could not understand.

13

4 What was town life like?

From 1485 to 1714 towns changed a lot. They got bigger, especially London. We will look at town life in the time of Queen Elizabeth I.

Towns were busy and exciting. They had markets, barbers, entertainments, shops and even schools. There was a lot to see and do. But towns did not have drains, rubbish collections, tap water or street lights. They were noisy, crowded and smelly.

Many poor people came to the towns to look for work. Often they did not find any. So they had to beg or steal to keep alive.

Source A

There was no tap water. People had to fetch their own water, or buy it from a water seller like the man in this picture. Often the water was taken straight from the river. People also threw their rubbish in the river.

Tudor towns did not have drains. People threw their dirty water and other rubbish into the street or into the river.

Tudor towns did not have tap water. People took their water from the river. Sometimes they bought their water from a water seller. This water came from the river too.

Tudor towns did not have street lights. People walked the streets in the dark or stayed indoors. People who had enough money could pay a man carrying a lamp to walk with them.

Source B   Town Councils tried to look after the streets, but mostly failed. Some main streets were cleaned and some were paved, but most streets were just like open sewers.

Written by a modern historian.

A modern artist's idea of what an Elizabethan street looked like. The shops looked on to the street. Each shop had a big window shutter which folded down to make a counter.

Rich people lived in large houses, with many rooms. They spent their time eating, drinking, going shopping, or amusing themselves.

Most of the other people in the town had to work. **Craftworkers** lived and worked in the same building. The ground floor of the house was the workshop and shop. Everyone in the town with the same trade had to join a **guild**. So shoemakers would have had a guild of their own, which they paid to join. Members of the guilds would each have an **apprentice**. The apprentice lived with the family to learn the trade.

Source D

A typical Elizabethan room, from a modern museum.

Source E

Most houses are wooden. Roofs are tiled or thatched. Floors are made of stone or plaster. The walls are plastered and painted or covered with cloths or tapestries. Rich people now have stoves. Glass is used more for windows, not polished horn or woven reeds. Houses have more chimneys, more rooms and more furniture.

Written in 1577 by William Harrison. He wrote a book about England at this time.

Source F

Poorer people eat chicken, milk, butter and cheese. The rich eat beef, venison, game birds and fish. They eat all they want. There is always something left and the servants eat that. If there is any left after this it is given to the poor. Rich people eat from silver or pewter, not wood. They drink from silver, pewter or glass.

Written by William Harrison in 1577.

Source G

People once ate breakfast, lunch at noon, dinner at five and supper before they went to bed. Now most people miss breakfast, eat dinner at eleven in the morning and supper at five. The poor eat what and when they can.

Written by William Harrison 1577.

An apprentice had to sign an agreement with his master. The master would feed him, give him clothes and train him in a trade. In return the apprentice worked for the master and had to obey rules such as:
- no marrying while an apprentice
- no gambling or drinking
- no selling of anything he has made.

When the apprenticeship was finished, the apprentice had to work as a **journeyman** for his master, for one more year.

Beggers all.

There are poor people everywhere. The rich should look after them. There are three sorts of poor: those who are poor because of a disaster, those who are poor because they cannot work and those who are poor because they will not work.

Written by William Harrison in 1577.

We should stop the building of houses in London for renting out. Many people are crowded into them. Up to twenty people have been found living in one room. These buildings are also badly built and cared for.

A letter written in 1590 to the Privy Council, who advised Elizabeth I.

▲ Some beggars, drawn at the time.

The poor and the law

Some town Councils had their own plans to help the poor. This was because the problem was worse in the towns. The Councils asked for money from people who were able to pay. This was then given to the poor.

Government laws about the poor saw them as three types, like those in Source I. It took the government a long time to see that some fit people were not working because they could not find work. At first the government punished fit people who were not working. Later they changed the law to try to give them work.

Were things different then?

Town life was very different for different sorts of people. The rich people in Source C are shown going out to enjoy themselves. Rich people had enough money and time to enjoy the good things about town life.

The beggar boy behind the rich people in Source C was living quite a different life. Beggars very often did not have homes to go to, and they did not have enough money for food, let alone fine clothes or trips to the theatre.

Most people who lived in towns had enough to eat and a place to live, but had to work hard for a living. These were people like the innkeeper and the fish seller in Source C.

5 Elizabethan country life

Most towns got bigger in Elizabethan times. Even so, most people still lived in the countryside.

Most villages had at least one blacksmith, brewer and baker. Each village had a church, or was close to one. People grew enough food to feed the village. If they grew more food or made more things than they needed, or needed things they could not make, they went to the nearest market town to trade.

Source B

The people in the village needed each other. This does not mean they always got on. They got drunk, fought, argued over land, sometimes stole from each other. From time to time they even killed each other. The poor poached from the rich, the rich worked the poor too hard.

From a modern book about the village of Terling in Tudor and Stuart times.

Source A

A modern artist's idea of what an Elizabethan village looked like.

Most people had more than one job. They worked in the fields and then made extra money from any other skill that they had. So Matthew Mitchell of Terling was a labourer, brewer and tailor.

From a modern book about the village of Terling in Tudor and Stuart times.

People in Terling grew wheat, kept animals and had orchards and gardens. They could feed themselves on their own grain, meat, milk, butter and cheese.

From a modern book about the village of Terling in Tudor and Stuart times.

The village used in many of the written sources in this unit is Terling in Essex, near Chelmsford. People still live there today.

A survey of Essex, written in 1597, said that Terling was in a 'very pleasant and commodious' place. The soil was good for growing crops. The River Ter ran through the middle of it, and there were plenty of wells and springs which provided water. Terling was close to Chelmsford, Witham and Braintree which held markets. It was also close to Maldon, which was a port used by ships carrying corn to London. This meant that any extra corn it grew could be easily sold at the markets, or in London.

Life in the countryside was changing. People had farmed by dividing the fields into **strips.** The strips were farmed by different people. This meant that everyone got strips of good and bad land. By Elizabeth I's time some people were joining the strips together and making separate fields. They **enclosed** (fenced off) these fields. This was not the only change. Many big land owners changed from growing corn to keeping sheep. They got more money for wool than for corn. They also needed fewer workers, so had to pay less in wages.

Source E

An Elizabethan shepherd.

Source F

Sheep have eaten up our Meadows and our downs, Our corn, our wood, whole Villages and towns.

From one of many songs about the change to sheep farming made up at the time.

Source G

In the time of Queen Elizabeth I the population of England grew. So did the population of the village of Terling. No one was forced to leave the village because of enclosure or sheep farming. But a lot of people still had to leave just to find work.

From a modern book about the village of Terling in Tudor and Stuart times.

Source H

In a village which once had over a hundred people there are now only a shepherd and his sheep. The villagers have no homes. They go looking for work. The same is happening everywhere. They can find no work. So they beg. Some steal, and are hanged for it.

From a letter written to King Henry VIII. The letter was against enclosing fields and changing from wheat to sheep farming.

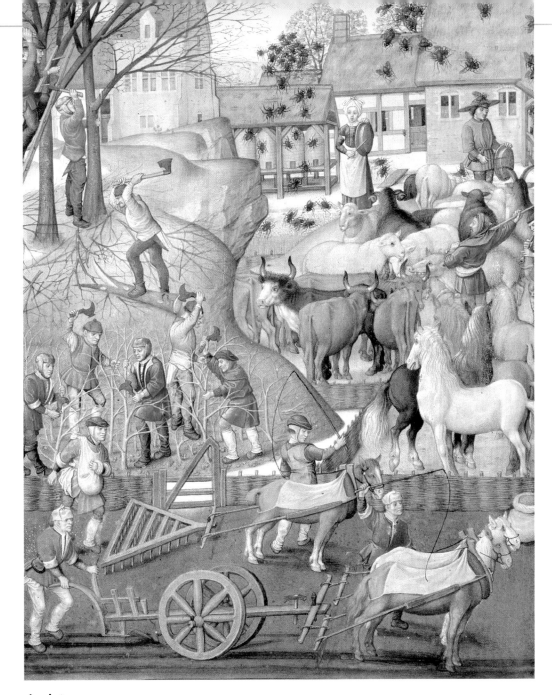

A picture showing a variety of farming jobs in Tudor times.

Population of London

1500   50,000

1714   700,000

(That is fourteen times as many people.)

Population of England, Wales, Scotland and Ireland

1500   3.75   million

1714   10.75 million

(That is just over three times as many people.)

Source J

Most village houses in 1485 had one floor, with one or two rooms. They were made from the cheapest local building materials. They had no chimney, or kitchen. The windows were holes that could be covered by wooden shutters.

The villagers had very few things. Wills show that a mattress, some clothing and bedding, a folding table, a bench or stools and a few wooden or leather dishes were all that most people had.

Written by a modern historian.

Source K

Wills from about 1597 show that beds were becoming more common for ordinary people. Bedding and clothes were important enough to be listed in wills, and given to particular people. Most families had a chest or two to store things in. At this time people were beginning to use 'proper' tables and chairs, rather than folding tables and benches. Perhaps this was because they had more space.

From a modern book about the village of Terling in Tudor and Stuart times.

Source L

Ploughing before Tudor times.

A map made in 1597 shows that most of the houses were just one storey, often just one room. There was sometimes a room added to one end of the house. Most houses had chimneys to take the smoke away.

From a modern book about the village of Terling in Tudor and Stuart times.

How did things change?

There were several changes in the countryside.

- Many farmers changed from farming small strips of land to farming enclosed fields.
- Many farmers changed from growing corn to keeping sheep, which meant that they needed fewer people to work for them.
- There were many more people who were out of work and homeless.
- People who still had jobs often found that their lives changed for the better. Their homes were more comfortable, and they could afford more furniture and other things for the house.

6 Entertainment in Shakespeare's time

How did people enjoy themselves in Shakespeare's time? Shakespeare was a famous playwright. He wrote most of his plays during the reign of James I. How people enjoyed themselves then depended on who they were, and where they lived.

The King and the people who lived with him, his **Court**, spent a lot of money on entertainment. **Masques** were written for them (masques were like modern musicals). Often they acted the parts themselves. They wore expensive costumes and make-up. There were also huge feasts and dances.

Towns had many shows, especially London, which had several theatres. Towns with no theatres used the yard of the biggest inn. Theatres were used for plays, and also by magicians and acrobats. At home, people liked to play cards, chess and draughts.

This is a costume for a masque by a famous designer called Inigo Jones. He also designed buildings for James I.

A masque in a country house in about 1610.

The house in Source C is supposed to be the house of Sir Henry Unton who was the son of a gentleman. He went to Oxford, studied law and travelled abroad in France and Italy.

He fought against the Spanish in the Netherlands in 1586.

Sir Henry was also an MP, and the Queen's Ambassador to France. On his second visit to France he was taken ill and died.

From a picture painted for Sir Henry Unton in 1596.

A modern artist's idea of what a play in a London theatre
would have looked like at the time of King James I.

Source E

If you stand below you only pay a penny. If you want to sit in the comfortable seats it costs another penny. During the performance food and drink are taken around the audience.

Written in 1599 by Thomas Platter in his book *Travels in England*.

Source F

I was at a theatre in Venice and saw a comedy acted. The theatre was not as grand as ours. The actors were not as well dressed as ours. The music was not as good as ours. I saw a woman act, a thing I never saw before.

Written in 1611 by Thomas Coryat in his book *Crudities*.

Scenery

There was a lot less scenery and fewer props than we have today. Lots of the scene setting came in what the actors were saying, to help the audience imagine the scene.

Here are some examples of this kind of scene setting:

"So this is the forest of Arden..."
"I see a rocky island..."
"The waves are high, the wind howls..."
"This bank is covered with flowers"
"What ugly hag is this..."

Today we sit quietly in a dark theatre, and listen carefully to every word of the play. In Shakespeare's time:

- there was no special stage lighting;
- people ate, drank and talked to each other during the performance;
- people joined in the performance. They booed the villains, cheered the heros, or threw food at actors who were acting badly.

Source G

1	rock	1	globe
1	cage	1	sceptre
2	tombs	1	lion
2	coffins	2	lions' heads
1	bed	1	snake
1	helmet	4	crowns
8	lances	1	ghost's crown
3	clubs	10	sets of stockings
1	shield	16	jackets
1	wooden hatchet	17	dresses (4 have been lost)
1	leather hatchet	14	cloaks

A list of some of the props (equipment and costumes) of a London theatre.

In the country people had outdoor amusements. Rich people hunted or fished. Travelling actors came to their homes. People played football and practiced archery. There were yearly fairs and celebrations.

Source **H**

King James produced a *Book of Sports* in 1618, which was read aloud after the Sunday church service. It said that Sunday entertainments after church were not wrong, as some people said. It said that people needed the exercise and change after working all week.

Written by a modern historian.

Source **I**

Sometimes necks are broken, sometimes backs. Sometimes arms are put out of joint, or legs. Sometimes their noses run with blood. There are no rules that I can tell. The man with the ball must run with it for his life.

Philip Stubbes writing about football in 1583. He was a Puritan and felt that people thought too much about fun on Sundays, and not enough about God.

Source **J**

The Cotswold Games – a yearly fair.

These are some games that children played at the time.

Were things different then?

Many games that children played in Shakespeare's time are still played today (see Source K). We still enjoy the theatre, music and dancing, and football.

One big difference is that in Shakespeare's time there were far more 'blood sports'; sports in which animals were hurt or killed. We still have fox hunting, but at that time they also had:

- bear baiting (a bear fought many dogs).
- cock fighting (cockerels fought each other).
- bull baiting (a bull fought many dogs).

7 How transport changed

The way that people travelled changed between 1485 and 1714. There were more types of transport in 1714, and more people were travelling. Coaches pulled by horses were used more and more. They were very uncomfortable on the bumpy roads, and had to be improved. In Stuart times there were many horse-drawn coach services, like our bus or train services today. People even wrote and published books showing the best routes around the country. Maps were more carefully drawn and became more accurate. But travelling was still difficult and, whether by sea or by land, dangerous.

Source C

Source D

Source A

In 1485 roads were bad. People either rode or walked. Carts were used if there was no other way to move something. They often got stuck in muddy or rutted roads.

Written by a modern historian.

Source B

Sir Christopher Wren mended the road near Whitehall in London. It had been badly kept and was muddy and full of holes. He dug down some two foot. Then he put layers of tar and earth down, until the road was level again. Now it is good. It only needs mending in bad weather and where the coaches have worn it out.

Written in 1696.

Different ways of travelling, from a painting made in 1520.

The different sorts of transport in the sources on this page:

Source A	Source B	Source C	Source D
horse	coach	sedan chair	coach
walking		horse	walking
cart		walking	cart

Fish Street, London, in about 1700.

Ships changed more than any other form of transport. This was partly because ship design was important in wars. If ships were designed well, they won more battles. It was also because people travelled more by sea, over longer distances, to trade and explore.

People wanted to trade with other countries. They had travelled over land to trade with countries like India and China. But land routes were long and difficult. There were often wars, which stopped traders moving about. Sea routes would be easier. People also wanted to explore. They wanted to find new lands to trade with. They wanted to own these lands too.

Source E

21 April: I think I will build a coach house and a stable, and have a coach of my own. I can afford it. I am almost ashamed to be seen travelling in a hired coach.

24 April: I went by water at ten at night to the Swan Inn.
I walked home from there at midnight.

Written in 1667 by Samuel Pepys, who lived in London.

Source F

Early traders in Venice, Italy, painted in about 1400. River travel was common in England too, especially in cities which had rivers running through them.

Trading ships in Bristol in the early 1700s.

Ship design

Good ship design was one of the things that helped the English to beat the Spanish Armada (see Unit 9). Good ship design made a ship fast and easy to manoeuvre.

Navigation

People had always used the stars to navigate. They also used very rough and inaccurate maps.

During Tudor and Stuart times map-making became much more accurate. Instruments were invented and improved to help navigation by the stars, and also without them.

Trade was important in Tudor and Stuart times. English people wanted **cloths**, like silk. They wanted **spices**, like cinnamon, pepper and cloves. They wanted sugar and lemons. In Stuart times people started to drink hot chocolate, coffee and tea. These things were not grown or made in England. People had to trade English things for them. People mostly traded wool for these goods.

Traders often made a lot of money. They charged very high prices for the goods they brought home. They took big risks. A whole cargo of spices or silks would be lost if a ship sank. The right to trade with foreign countries was so important that wars were fought over it. The English and Dutch fought three separate wars over trade in 1652, 1665 and 1672.

A cup made for holding spices from the Indies.

The Royal Exchange

The Royal Exchange was where merchants from all over the world met. They talked and traded with each other. It was a large building with a big central courtyard, where most people met. It was damaged in the Great Fire of 1666, although the parts made of stone survived. It was re-built by 1671. It was so important to trade in England that it was one of the first big public buildings to be finished.

**Source
H** At the Change I heard two rich ships have come home, which were feared sunk. Sir Thomas Chamberlain showed me letters from the East Indies. They show how the Dutch behave. They are rude to all English, even the people at our only trading post there. They beat several men, and hung our flag under theirs. They say they will be masters of all the southern seas.

Written in 1664 by Samuel Pepys. The Change was the Royal Exchange, a building where most London trading went on.

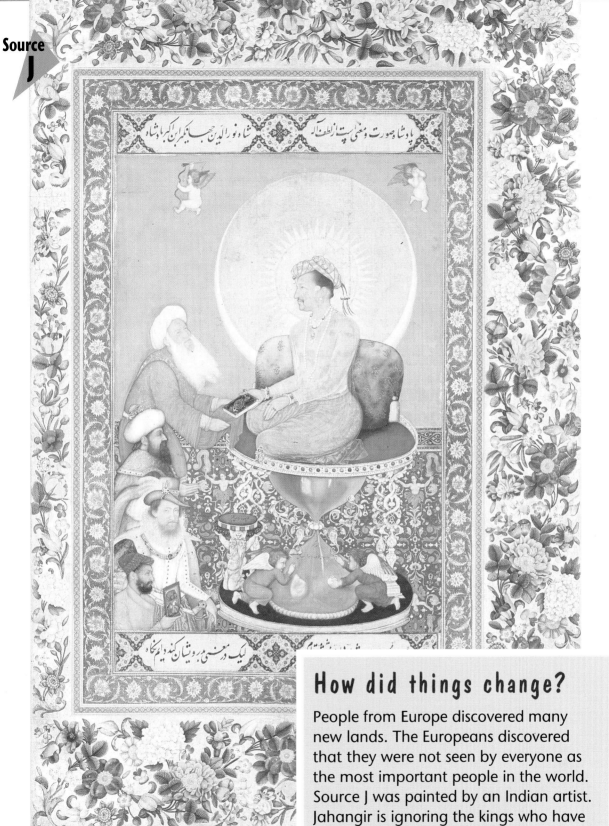

This painting shows the Indian emperor, Jahangir, being given presents by European kings. One of them is supposed to be James I.

How did things change?

People from Europe discovered many new lands. The Europeans discovered that they were not seen by everyone as the most important people in the world. Source J was painted by an Indian artist. Jahangir is ignoring the kings who have come to bring him presents. The artist wanted to show that Jahangir was more important than these kings.

8 The privateers: heroes or pirates?

When Elizabeth I was Queen, many English seamen went
exploring. They found new places, and new things to trade.
Walter Raleigh brought back potatoes and tobacco from America.
He also tried to set up the first English settlement there. Francis
Drake made a voyage right around the world looking for new
places to trade with.

There were trade routes set up to China, India, Africa, Russia and
America.

The merchants brought back silk from China, spices from India,
slaves and spices from Africa, furs from Russia and gold and
pearls from America.

Source A

**A map made in 1587. You can see Drake's route
around the world.**

The seamen making these voyages also fought the Spanish. They called themselves **privateers**. This meant that although they were not in the navy, the government said they could attack enemy ships. Much of the treasure they brought home came from Spanish ships they sank, or Spanish towns they raided, not from trade. The English thought they were helping their country. The Spanish saw them as pirates. Can we tell who was right?

Source B

Many people became rich through trade. John Hawkins, one of the privateers, had trouble with his first trade voyage. He made nothing. On his second voyage, selling African slaves in America, he made a huge profit.

Written by a modern historian.

Source C

I have heard exactly what the English have been doing in America. They have sailed into the harbours and traded all their things. Some of this has been done in a friendly way. Sometimes they have used force, and stolen all they could, far more than their things were worth.

Written by a German trader, living in Spain at the time.

Drake's voyage around the world

Dec. 1577:   Left Plymouth with five ships.

Oct. 1578:   Reached Chile, in South America. Just one ship, the *Golden Hind*, left.

Dec. 1578:   Captured Spanish gold.

July 1579:   Claimed California for England.

Oct. 1579:   Made trade treaty with Ternate (an island off the coast of Asia). Left with six tons of spice.

Feb. 1580   *Golden Hind* stuck on a sandbank. Spice thrown overboard to lose weight.

Sept. 1580:   Home to England with Spanish gold.

Drake's voyage around the world gave opportunites for piracy, exploration and trade.

Piracy
Capture of Spanish gold, December 1578.

Exploration
Claiming of California, July 1579.

Trade
Treaty with Ternate, October 1579.

The spices had to be thrown overboard and California could not be brought home. The gold was the only obvious gain from the voyage.

Source

D In 1494, the Pope said the New World (America) was to be divided between Spain and Portugal. He said no other country could settle there, or trade with the people. No one else could have their gold.

Written by a modern historian.

Source

E In 1562 John Hawkins made his first trading voyage. He bought African slaves and arranged with the Spanish to sell them in America. He bought pearls, sugar and gold. He sent them back to England by way of Seville. The Spanish took them. They did not reply to letters from Queen Elizabeth asking for them to be given back.

Written by a modern historian.

Source

F

Source G

Englishmen have robbed our merchant ships. They have taken everything. We have lost a lot. We have sent letters to the Queen of England to complain. Nothing has happened.

Written from Spain to the Spanish Ambassador in England.

Source H

Francis Drake has returned from the Indies. He captured several of our towns. He brought back 140 cannons and ammunition for them, about £1,000 worth of pearls, over £70,000 worth of gold and silver, and some other stuff.

I cannot send news of when the English ships might set out on another raid. Ships are leaving all the ports all the time, and there is no way of knowing where they are going to. Our ships should travel in groups. Even if they had to pay armed ships to guard them it would be worth it.

Written in 1586 by a Spanish spy in England.

◄ A drawing of Drake's raid on the Spanish town of Santiago in 1585.

What do people say about the past?

You have seen that people in Elizabethan times disagreed about whether the privateers were heroes or pirates. Even modern historians have different views about the privateers. Different people use different pieces of evidence to show their views of the story.

We have concentrated on Drake in this unit. Other privateers were:

- Martin Frobisher
- Richard Grenville
- John Hawkins
- John Norris
- Walter Raleigh

All of these men were knighted at some time by Queen Elizabeth I. This may well show what her view of them was.

9 Why did the Armada fail?

In the summer of 1588 Philip II of Spain sent 130 ships, the **Armada**, to attack England. The plan was to meet a Spanish army at Calais and take it across the Channel to invade England. Everyone expected the plan to work.

As soon as the Armada reached the Channel the English ships attacked. The Armada carried on up the Channel. It sailed at the speed of the slowest ship. The English kept on attacking, but they could not stop it. It took four days to reach Calais, but the Armada had only lost two ships when it got there.

While the Armada was at Calais the English set fire to eight of their old ships. They sailed these **fireships** into the middle of the Armada. The Spanish panicked. Many captains cut away their anchors to escape quickly. The English were waiting to attack. They damaged many Spanish ships with cannon fire. Then there was a storm. The Armada was split up. It could not keep together, or anchor, or meet the army now. So the Spanish decided to go home another way, around the tip of Scotland and Ireland. Only 40 ships got back to Spain in late September.

This picture was painted about twenty years after the Armada sailed. Many Spanish ships were high at the back. This made them hard to sail in a strong wind. Some of the Spanish crew were not sailors. They had not been trained to fire cannons quickly. Some English ships were much lower at the back. This made them easier to sail. The English crews were all well trained.

Source

B

My health is bad and I know that I am always sea sick. The Armada is so big and so important that the person in charge should understand navigation and sea fighting, and I know nothing of either.

Part of a letter to King Philip II of Spain, from the man he chose to lead the Armada. Philip still chose him.

Armada timetable, 1588.

21 July: Armada leaves Spain.

29 July: Armada seen from the end of Cornwall.

31 July – 6 August: Fighting in the Channel.

6 August: Armada at Calais.

7/8 August: Fireship attack.

8 August: Battle at Gravelines.

9 August: Storm.

21 September: Armada back in Spain.

This is a painting of the fireships at Calais.
Fireships were old ships which were set on fire
and sailed towards the enemy.

**Source
F**

An English medal, made after
the Armada was beaten. The
words around the edge say 'God
breathed, and they were
scattered'. This is referring to the
storm which damaged the Armada
after it left Calais.

**Source
D** They have a captain for their ship, a
captain for their guns and a captain for each
group of soldiers. This leads to great
confusion.

**Written by a captain of one of the English
ships which fought against the Armada.**

**Source
E** Whenever we fired a cannon we had
at least an hour's work to load it again.

**Written by a sailor on a Spanish ship
during a battle in 1589.**

Why did things happen?

People argue over why the Armada failed. Here are some causes that they give. A **cause** is something that makes things happen.

- The **design** of the ships of both sides. The English ships could sail better. (L)
- The **training** of both crews. The Spanish had not been trained to keep loading and firing cannons. The English had. (L)
- Spanish **cannons** were long, heavy, difficult to re-load. English cannons were shorter and easier to move. (L)
- The **fireships**. These caused the panic at Calais, and split up the Armada for the English to fire at. (S)
- The **weather**. This was very bad. It affected both sides, but the English could shelter in English ports. (S)
- The plan was too complicated. It meant the Armada had to meet a land army, a long way from Spain, at an exact time. This was never likely to be easily done. (S)

> **Types of Cause**
> Long-term: These grew over a
>   long time.
> Short-term: These happened
>   more suddenly.

The letters L and S in brackets at the end of each cause tell you what sort they were.

Source G

Many of the enemy's ships were better than us in battle. Better designed, with better guns, gunners, and crew. If on the day we arrived at Calais the army had come we could have won.

Written by Don Francisco de Bobilla, commander of the soldiers on board the Armada.

10 Was Guy Fawkes framed?

On 5 November 1605 Guy Fawkes was caught trying to blow up King James I and Parliament. He was found in a cellar under the House of Lords. He was just about to set light to 36 barrels of gunpowder. Fawkes was arrested and tortured. He said there had been other people in the plot. A search was made for the rest of the plotters. Some were killed trying to escape. The rest were questioned, tried, and found guilty. They were hanged.

The government said they had found out about the plot when a Catholic lord was sent a letter telling him to stay away from Parliament. He gave the letter to **Robert Cecil**, James I's chief minister. Cecil told King James. They sent some soldiers to the cellar and caught Guy Fawkes. But there are some things about the story that make some people ask the question 'Was Guy Fawkes framed?'

Source A

It has pleased God to uncover a plot to kill the King, Queen, Prince and the most important men of this land by secretly putting much gunpowder into a cellar under Parliament, and blowing them all up at once.

Written by Robert Cecil to the English Ambassador in Brussels on 9 November 1605.

Source B

We cannot hope to run the country while many people obey foreign rulers. This is what Catholics do. The priests tell them that they must do everything to help their religion, even killing the King.

Robert Cecil is supposed to have said this.

Source C

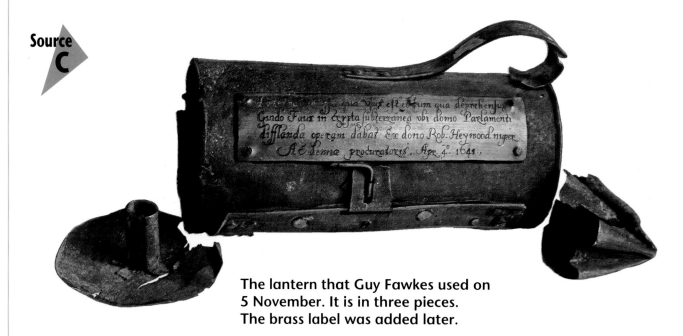

The lantern that Guy Fawkes used on 5 November. It is in three pieces. The brass label was added later.

Diſſlo Diſſipo
I blow and ſcatter
Ick blaes en verſtroy

88

Ventorum
Ludibrium

VIDEO RIDEO

I ſee and ſmile

Opus tenebrarum
A deed of darknes

Novemb. yͤ 5ᵗʰ

In perpetuam Papiſtarum infamiam

In foveam quam foderit

Faux

Duanthillum abſum
Hoc nae
How nye

Invented by Samuell Ward
preacher of Ipſwich

Source D

This print was made just after the Gunpowder Plot. The Armada is out at sea to the left. The Pope and the Devil are plotting in the tent. The Pope was Head of the Catholic Church.

The plotters

The usual story of the Gunpowder Plot is that the plot was discovered at the last minute. Often the only plotter that you hear about is Guy Fawkes. He was a soldier who had spent a long time fighting in Italy. He sometimes called himself Guido (which is the Italian for Guy). When he was first captured in the cellar he said his name was Johnson.

There were, in fact, several other plotters. Most of them, apart from Guy Fawkes, were related to the man who led the plot, Thomas Percy. He was a Catholic gentleman. He wanted to kill King James I so that he could be replaced by a Catholic monarch.

Guy Fawkes was tortured. He told his torturers the names of the rest of the plotters. They were hunted down. Some of them were shot trying to escape. One died in prison in the Tower of London. Eight were tried and executed for High Treason.

Source E

I hear that the Privy Council and some Lords were in Parliament and a barrel of gunpowder was lit under them. And that it went off, and most, if not all of them were blown up. I cannot believe so strange and desperate an act.

Written by a person living in Paris, to a friend in England in 1605.

This memorial to the Gunpowder Plot was painted in 1630. It shows God
protecting the royal family, and punishing the plotters.

Source G

The Captain and I sat up late drinking and watching the boys in the street throwing fireworks. Today has been a holiday all through the City.

Written by Samuel Pepys in his diary on 5 November, 1661.

Source H

Those people who know how the government do things are sure that this is a trap, and that some members of the Privy Council have tricked these men.

Written by a Catholic visitor to England, in 1605.

Source I

Shocked by the Gunpowder Plot, the King and Parliament made laws against Catholics.

Written by a modern historian.

Source J

The usual story is that the plot really was discovered at the last minute. Others say it was a plot by Cecil to make James act against the Catholics. We can never know for sure.

A modern historian, writing about the Gunpowder Plot.

More information

Many people were worried that James I was not hard enough on the Catholics.

Robert Cecil was in charge of security. He could get into the Tower of London very easily.

Gunpowder was not something that you could just buy. All of the gunpowder in England was kept in the Tower of London.

Lists were kept of everything in the Tower of London. The lists for 1604 are missing.

How do we know?

Most historians agree that we cannot know if Guy Fawkes was framed without more evidence. The sources that we have can be looked at in different ways.

Historians who want to believe that Cecil framed Fawkes and the others to get James I to act against the Catholics would use Sources B, H and I to support their views. They would say that the plotters could not have got the gunpowder without getting into the Tower of London, which Cecil controlled.

Historians who argue with this might say the gunpowder could have been sent by Catholics from another country and that the author of Source H is a Catholic and would therefore be lying.

11 How did people fight in the Civil War?

The Civil War began in 1642. The **Royalists** and the **Parliamentarians** fought each other over the way the country should be run. They had no modern weapons. They fought with pikes, muskets and cannons.

Pikes were very long spears. **Pikemen** always fought together in large groups, called **hedgehogs**.

Musketeers used a gun, called a musket. They carried gunpowder and a lighted fuse all the time. Muskets could kill from further away than pikes, but they took a long time to load and fire.

Pikemen and musketeers were called 'foot', because they fought together on foot. The other part of the army, the horsemen, were called 'horse'. The horsemen fought with pistols and swords.

Source A

A modern artist's idea of what a Civil War battle looked like.

Battles were confusing. It was hard to tell the sides apart because their clothes were similar. At the battle of Edgehill the sides used different coloured sashes to tell each other apart. Sir Faithful Fortescue's men changed sides. They forgot to take off their Parliamentarian sashes. Many of them were shot by the men they had just joined.

Written by a modern historian.

Pikes were between four to six metres long. Pikemen often cut down their pikes to make them easier to use. A pikeman had to be strong to use a pike, and to wear the heavy armour. He had a helmet and armour to cover his body, neck and thighs.

Written by a modern historian.

The Armies used various methods to tell each other apart.
Passwords: these were chosen before a battle. At Edgehill the Royalist password was 'For God and King Charles'. This would have been easy to guess! It could easily have been heard in battle.
Signs: a sign that the Parliamentarians used in battle was to place a piece of paper in their hats. But what if they lost them, or the paper got muddy?
Sashes: Royalist sashes were red, Parliamentarian sashes were orange. These colours are quite similar and could easily have got mixed up.

All of the written sources on these pages are about the first real battle of the Civil War, at **Edgehill** in 1642. The battle started at midday and ended when it got too dark to fight. No one had won, the battle just stopped, and the soldiers moved on.

Source D

From a stained glass window made soon after the Civil War, in memory of some of the soldiers who fought in it.

Source E

We fired our cannons, and our horsemen charged. The enemy ran. We chased them for four miles. Many of them escaped by guessing our password, which was 'For God and King Charles'. The battle stopped when it grew dark. We killed many of their men. Even more have run away and will not come back.

Written by a Royalist horseman.

Source F

Both armies began by firing their cannons. Our horseman charged theirs, and chased them for two to three miles. But the chase lost us the chance to win. Our horsemen did not come back to break up the enemy's foot soldiers. When the musketeers' ammunition was gone the pikemen fought. The King's flag was captured. We got it back at last, and the horsemen came back, but by then it was too late to fight any longer.

Written by a Royalist horseman.

Source G

From a film about the Civil War, made in 1970.

Source

H   They had more men than we expected. They had many horsemen. They had nine big groups of foot. After some cannon firing their horsemen charged us, and then the foot soldiers closed in. Our men were so fierce that the enemy musketeers hid behind their pikemen, rather than shoot at us. Many of the King's men ran away. Then it got dark. We had used all our ammunition, so we let them leave the battlefield.

Written by a Parliamentarian soldier.

Source

I   We are tired out from keeping watch for so many nights. It was a long fight, too. It lasted from noon till dusk. No one was fed that night. I could not find my servant, who had my cloak. I had nothing to keep me warm, so I had to walk about all night. It was a cold night, with a sharp frost.

Written by a Parliamentarian soldier.

How do we know?

The sources that we have are mostly written sources. As most people took sides at the time, these written sources will be biased towards one side or the other. That means we have to think carefully about what people are saying in them.

Sources for what it was like to fight include the armour they wore and the weapons they held. There are also paintings of supposed officers from both sides which show them ready for battle. These paintings cannot show us what ordinary soldiers wore.

The stained glass window, Source D, is in St. Chad's Church, Faringdon, Cheshire. The window was made in memory of the Royalist soldiers who fought in the Civil War.

12 Life in Pepys' London

Charles I lost the Civil War. In 1649 he was executed. England was run by Parliament, and then by **Oliver Cromwell**. The government was Puritan. It passed laws to stop people doing things it thought were wrong. These included going to the theatre. Even Christmas celebrations were banned.

Many people still wanted a king at the head of the government. Soon after Oliver Cromwell died, Charles II came back to England. It was 1660. Many people celebrated the **restoration** (bringing back) of the Stuarts. They hoped to restore things to the way they had been before the Civil War.

But things were different, and they carried on changing. London had a bad outbreak of sickness (the plague), and a huge fire, which destroyed much of the city. Architects had to redesign parts of the city. The new St Paul's Cathedral was designed by Christopher Wren.

Source A

This is a picture of a part of London which was rebuilt after the Great Fire of 1666.

Source B

All the talk nowdays is that the King will come again. It seems to me that everybody wishes it. I hope it will be so.

Written by Samuel Pepys. He kept a diary from 1660–1669, which tells us a lot about life in London at this time.

Source C

The King has agreed to the conditions, and is to return. Great joy all yesterday in London. Bells were rung, bonfires lit and people drank the King's health.

Written by Samuel Pepys.

How did things change?

This street is very different from the Elizabethan street on page 15.
The street is paved, and it is wider.
The buildings are made of stone.
The buildings are bigger.
People are dressed differently.
The pavement is marked off to separate people walking from carts and horses.

But:
The shops still front on to the street.
There are still no street lights.
People are still selling things from baskets.
This is a main street. Not all streets would have been like this. The side street to the left of the picture doesn't have a separate pavement, for example.

13 Plague!

The plague was spread by the fleas on rats biting people, putting the illness into their blood. People caught the plague all through Tudor and Stuart times. It was worse in the towns, where people were crowded together, and rats could live on the rubbish.

People did not know what caused plague, or how to stop it. All they knew was that it spread quickly, especially in hot weather, and that there was no known cure. One of the worst cases of the plague was the **Great Plague**, of 1665. It was very bad in London, where it killed over 100,000 people.

Symptoms of the plague

Temperature.
Headache.
Sickness.
Patient gets a lump (**buboe**) where the flea bite is.
The lump goes black.
Armpits, neck and legs get lumps.
Patient better after 10 days
OR
gets spots all over the skin, like bruises.
Patient dies.

Source B

22 July: There are not many people in London. I only met two coaches and two carts as I went home. Dr Burnett's servant died of a buboe and spots on his leg – that is the plague.

Written by Samuel Pepys, in 1665. He lived in London.

Source A

Dogs are killed. Great fires are made in the streets. People take medicines. None of this is sure to work.

Written in 1665 by William Petty, who was a scientist. He was writing about the plague.

In Source C the plague-cart men are ringing a hand bell. This was to warn people to get out of the way. It also told them to put the bodies of the dead out on to the street. They were not supposed to put the bodies out of the house until they heard the cart coming, although many of them did.

A modern artist's idea of the
plague carts collecting the dead.

Source D

A print made at the time of people burying plague bodies.

Source F

Searchers and doctors must check the sick and dead in each house for plague.

If there is plague in a house, the house, and the people in it, are shut up for a month after the last death there. The door of the house must be marked with a red cross and 'Lord Have Mercy Upon Us'.

Dead bodies must be buried two metres deep before sun-rise or after sun-set.

The streets must be kept clean. People are to be given the job of raking the rubbish away. Animals in the city are to be sent away or killed.

Government orders for London during the plague.

Source G

7 September: I went to St James. It was sad and dangerous to see so many coffins in the streets. There are few people about, the shops are shut up, no one knows who will be next.

Written by John Evelyn, in 1665. He lived in London, like Pepys.

Source E

7 June: Today I saw two or three houses with a red cross on the doors, and 'Lord Have Mercy Upon Us'. A sad sight, they are the first I have seen. I bought some tobacco to smell and chew.
20 July: My Lady Carteret gave me a bottle of plague cure to take home with me.

Written by Samuel Pepys, in 1665.

More information

Some people thought the plague was caused by bad air.

Some people thought it was caused by touching others.

Here are some things that people did to try to stop catching the plague:

- People lit bonfires in the streets to burn the bad air.
- People burnt herbs on the fire in sickrooms.
- People sucked tablets made of cinnamon and myrrh.

- People who had the plague had to stay at home. If they had no homes, they had to go to 'pest houses' where everyone had the plague.
- People would not go near houses where people had the plague.
- People burnt tar on the fire of the sickroom. This made a thick, black, bad smelling smoke.
- Money used in shops was put into bowls of vinegar, not passed from hand to hand.
- People drank sage, rue, buttercup, angelica roots and saffron mixed in sweet wine.

Source H

A plague doctor's outfit.

How do we know?

The Plague doctor's outfit shows that the doctors took no chances. If the plague was passed on by touch, they were not going to have any part of the patient touching their skin. In the case of bad air, the 'beak' of the peculiar mask was filled with herbs and spices, to filter the air.

We know how bad the Plague was because towns published 'Bills of Mortality' (lists of how many people had died) during plagues. These lists are not always accurate. Sometimes people managed to avoid having their houses shut up by calling a plague death something else.

14 Fire!

The Great Fire of London started on 2 September 1666, in Pudding Lane. Fires often happened in Tudor and Stuart times. Open fires were used for heating and cooking. Candles were used for lights. Accidents were likely with all these flames about. What was surprising about the Great Fire was how fast it spread, and how much of the city it burnt. Why was it such a bad fire?

To answer this question we have to look at the way that people fought fires at the time. We also need to look at how London was built. We are lucky to have the diary of Samuel Pepys, who was in London during the fire. He wrote down the things he saw and heard. This should give us some clues.

Source A

This is all that people had to fight the fire.

Source B

Jane woke us at three in the morning, to tell us of a great fire in the city. I went to her window. I thought it was far enough away and went back to bed. About seven I got up to dress, and looked out of the window. I saw the fire was dying out, and was further off.

Samuel Pepys writing in his diary on 2 September 1666.

Source C

Jane tells me that about 300 houses were burned down by the fire we saw. It is now burning down all of Fishstreet by London Bridge.

Samuel Pepys writing in his diary on 2 September 1666.

A modern artist's idea of what
it was like during the fire.

Source E

A Dutch artist painted this picture of the fire at the time.

Source F

Nobody was trying to put it out. They were all trying to save their things and escape. The wind is driving the fire towards the City. After so long without rain, everything burns very easily, even the stone churches.

Written by Samuel Pepys on 2 September 1666.

Source G

I told the King what I saw, and he told me to tell the Lord Mayor to pull down the houses all around the fire. I met the Lord Mayor, who said: "What can I do? I am worn out! People will not obey me. I have been pulling down houses. But the fire is quicker than we are."

Written by Samuel Pepys on 2 September 1666.

Source H

The houses are very close together, and full of things that burn well, like tar and oil and brandy. The streets were full of people and horses and carts loaded with things, ready to run one another over, moving things from one burning house to another.

Written by Samuel Pepys on 2 September 1666.

Source I

With your face in the wind you were almost burned with a shower of firedrops. Houses five or six houses apart were set alight with these flakes of fire.

Written by Samuel Pepys on 3 September 1666.

Now begins the blowing up of houses in Tower Street, next to the Tower. It stopped the fire where it was done, bringing down the houses to the ground, and then it was easy to put out Going to the fire I found that by blowing up of houses, and the work of the workmen out of the shipyards, there is a good stop to it.

Written by Samuel Pepys on 4 September 1666.

Why did things happen?

The fire spread so quickly because:
- Everything was very dry, because there had been no rain.
- Most of the buildings were made of wood and thatch, which burn easily.
- Many buildings near Pudding Lane had stores of things that burned easily.
- The wind was very strong, and blew bits of burning thatch quickly to other houses.
- No one was trying to put the fire out.
- There was really no proper fire-fighting equipment.

Part of a map made soon after the fire which shows the buildings that survived.

INDEX

abbeys 8
actors 26–29, 30
America 38, 39, 40
apprentice 16
Armada 42, 45, 47

baker 20
battles 50–53
beggars 14, 18–19, 22
blacksmith 20
brewer 20
buboe 56

carts 32
Catholics 8–13, 46, 47, 49
Cecil, Robert 46, 49
Charles I 52, 54
Charles II 54
chocolate 36
Civil War 11, 50–53, 54
coaches 32, 34
coffee 36
corn 22
countryside 20–25, 30
Court 26
craftworkers 16
Cromwell, Oliver 54

dances 26
divorce 8
Drake, Sir Francis 38, 39, 41

Edgehill, Battle of 51
Edward VI 10
Elizabeth I 11, 14, 18, 22, 38, 40
enclosure 22
entertainment 14, 26–27
exploration 34, 38, 39

fairs 30
farming 20–25
Fawkes, Guy 46–47
feasts 26

fire 54, 60–63
fireships 42, 44
fleas 56
food 16
football 30

Great Fire of London 54, 60–63
games 31
guilds 16

Hawkins, John 39, 40
Henry VIII 8, 22
horses 32
houses 16, 17, 18, 20–21, 24, 25

James I 26, 28, 30, 46

land journeys 34
Latin 8, 10
lemons 36
London 14, 26, 28, 32, 34, 54, 56, 58, 60–63

maps 32
market 14, 20
Mary I 11
masques 26, 27
monks 8, 9

nuns 8

parliament 46, 54
Parliamentarians 50, 51, 53
Pepys, Samuel 34, 36, 49, 54, 56, 58, 60, 62, 63
Philip II 42, 43
pirates 38, 39, 41
plague 54, 56, 57, 58, 59
plays 26
poor law 19
poor 14, 17, 18, 19
Pope 8, 10, 40, 47
Portugal 40
privateers 38, 39, 41
Privy Council 18, 47, 49

Protestants 10
Puritans 10, 30, 54

Queen Anne 11

Raleigh, Sir Walter 38
rats 56
reformation 8, 10
religion 8–13
restoration 54
rich 16, 17, 18, 30
roads 32
Royal Exchange 36
Royalists 50, 52

sea 34
seamen 38, 39
Shakespeare 26
sheep 22
shepherd 22
ship design 34, 42, 45
ships 34, 35
shops 14, 15, 16, 58
silk 36
slaves 40
Spain 40, 41, 42, 44
spices 36
sugar 36
Syon Abbey 8

tea 36
theatre 26, 29, 54
Tower of London 49
Town Councils 14, 19
towns 14, 16, 19, 20, 26
trade 16, 20, 34, 36, 39
transport 32, 34
travel 32–33
treasure 39

villages 20, 22, 24

wars 34, 36
weapons 50
wool 22, 36
work 16
workshops 16
Wren, Sir Christopher 32, 54